Usborne Guide to MODEL RAILWAYS

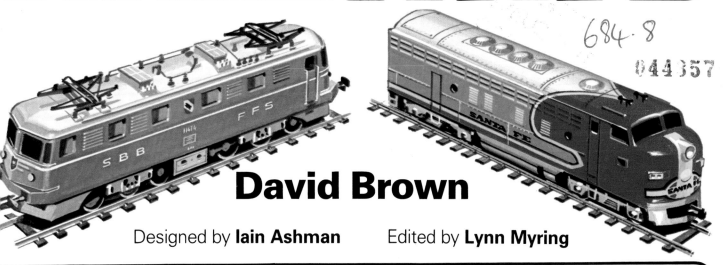

David Brown

Designed by **Iain Ashman**   Edited by **Lynn Myring**

CONTENTS

Illustrated by
**Basil Arm, Mike Roffe,
Swanston Associates,
Craig Warwick, Gordon Wylie.**

INTRODUCING MODEL RAILWAYS

This picture of part of a model railway layout shows some of the interesting features that you could include on your own railway. You can see large, very detailed layouts at model railway exhibitions. They are usually built specially for exhibitions by model railway clubs or model manufacturers. Looking at other people's railways will give you lots of ideas for building your own.

Looking around model shops will help you decide which things you can afford to buy and which things look simple enough to make yourself.

Rivers are quite easy to model and they provide a good reason for having a railway bridge. You can buy bridges ready-made, or in kits that you put together yourself. Fix them firmly into the ground as trains can become derailed on a shaky bridge. (See page 23 to find out how to model water.)

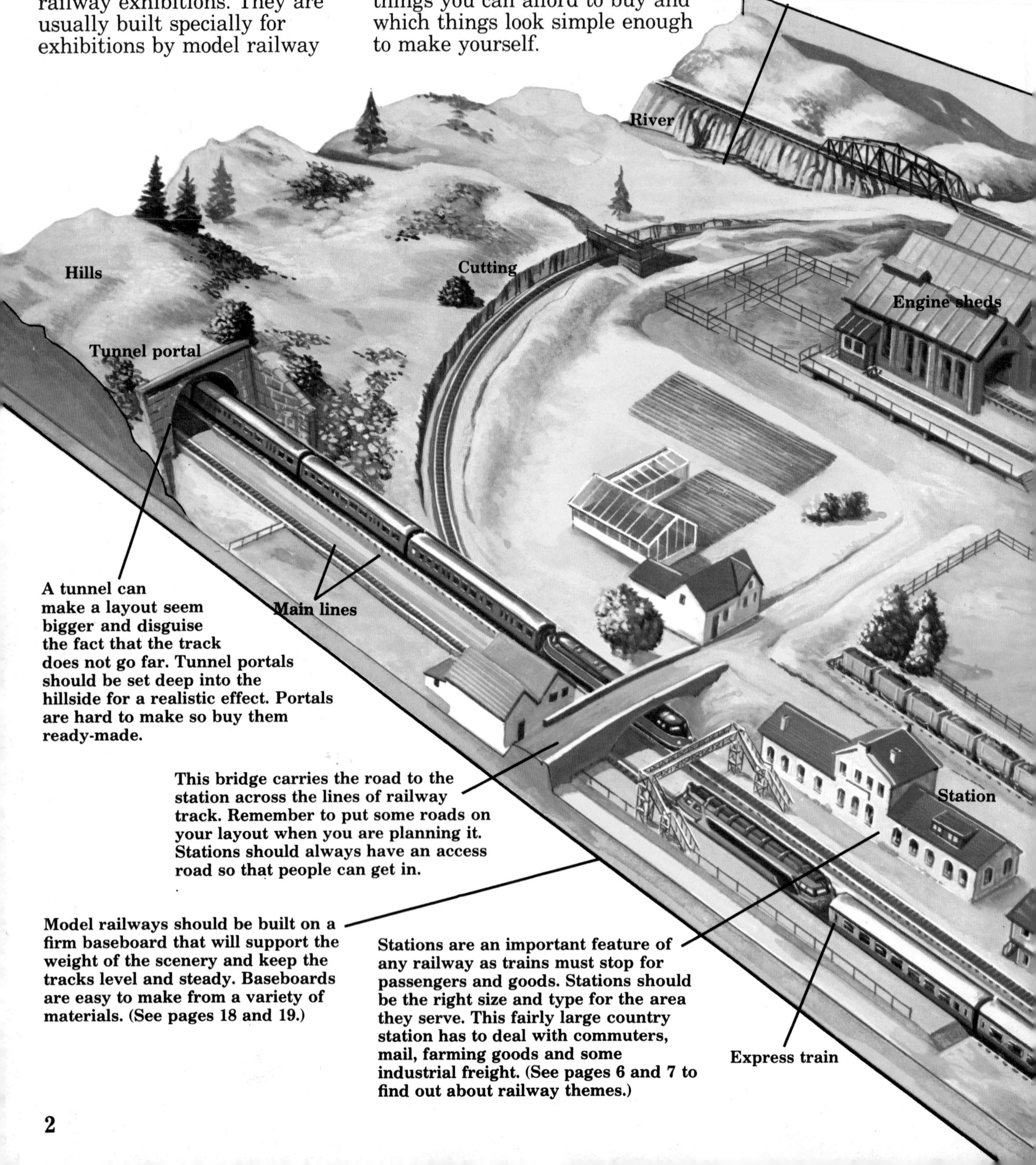

River

Hills

Cutting

Engine sheds

Tunnel portal

A tunnel can make a layout seem bigger and disguise the fact that the track does not go far. Tunnel portals should be set deep into the hillside for a realistic effect. Portals are hard to make so buy them ready-made.

Main lines

This bridge carries the road to the station across the lines of railway track. Remember to put some roads on your layout when you are planning it. Stations should always have an access road so that people can get in.

Station

Model railways should be built on a firm baseboard that will support the weight of the scenery and keep the tracks level and steady. Baseboards are easy to make from a variety of materials. (See pages 18 and 19.)

Stations are an important feature of any railway as trains must stop for passengers and goods. Stations should be the right size and type for the area they serve. This fairly large country station has to deal with commuters, mail, farming goods and some industrial freight. (See pages 6 and 7 to find out about railway themes.)

Express train

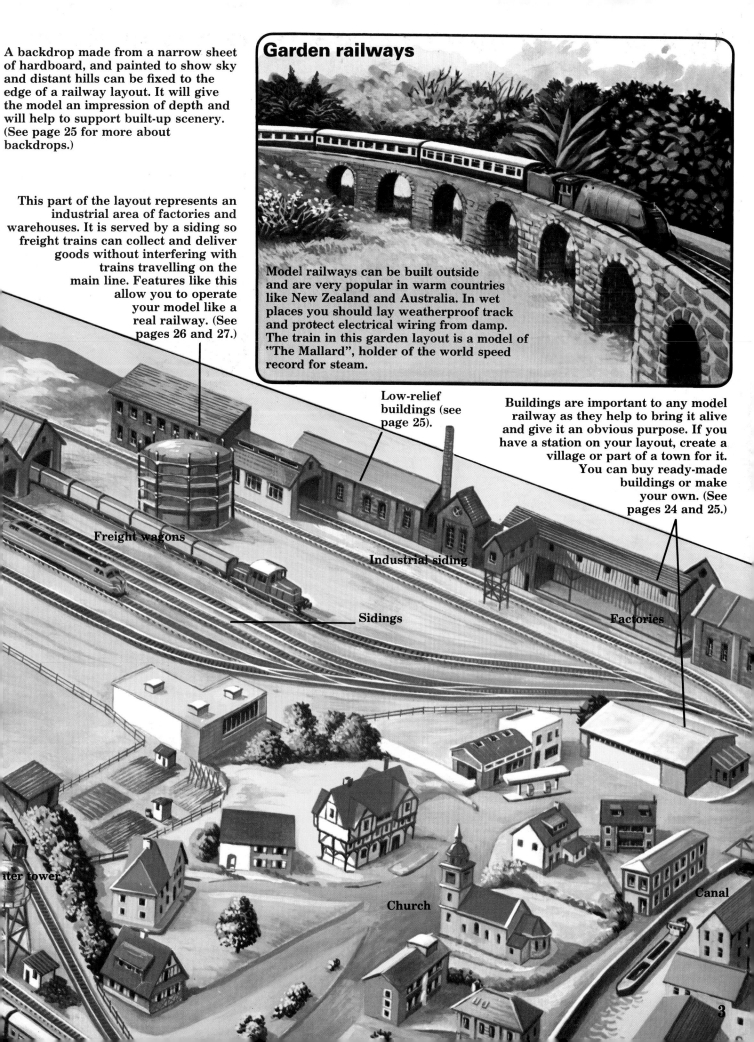

A backdrop made from a narrow sheet of hardboard, and painted to show sky and distant hills can be fixed to the edge of a railway layout. It will give the model an impression of depth and will help to support built-up scenery. (See page 25 for more about backdrops.)

This part of the layout represents an industrial area of factories and warehouses. It is served by a siding so freight trains can collect and deliver goods without interfering with trains travelling on the main line. Features like this allow you to operate your model like a real railway. (See pages 26 and 27.)

Garden railways

Model railways can be built outside and are very popular in warm countries like New Zealand and Australia. In wet places you should lay weatherproof track and protect electrical wiring from damp. The train in this garden layout is a model of "The Mallard", holder of the world speed record for steam.

Low-relief buildings (see page 25).

Buildings are important to any model railway as they help to bring it alive and give it an obvious purpose. If you have a station on your layout, create a village or part of a town for it. You can buy ready-made buildings or make your own. (See pages 24 and 25.)

Freight wagons

Industrial siding

Sidings

Factories

iter tower

Church

Canal

3

SCALE, GAUGE AND POWER

Two of the most important things to decide when planning a model railway layout are what size your models will be and how they will be powered.

The size of the layout as a whole will depend upon the space available to you. However, what you can show on the layout will depend upon the size of the models you choose. The main commercial sizes are explained in the diagrams and chart below. The most popular and convenient are HO and OO, which are similar in size, and N gauge which is very small and most useful if you do not have a lot of space.

Model power

Although most model trains are powered by electricity today, clockwork and live steam powered models are still available.

The train below is a live steam model. These are really miniature steam trains worked by small, but real, steam engines. Most steam trains are made in gauges 1 or O, as it is difficult to make a smaller working engine. They are often built by model engineers but some models, like the one shown below, can be made from a kit.

Scales and gauges

Scale describes the difference between the size of a model and the size of the real train that the model is based upon. Scale is often expressed in numbers as a ratio of the two sizes, such as 160:1. This means that 160mm of the real train is represented by 1mm of the model.

Gauge is the distance between the inside edges of the rails, as shown in the picture below. Models built to different scales usually run on different gauges but a few scales do use the same gauge width. (See chart on far right.)

Gauge

▲The rails of this track are 16.5mm apart. It is used by OO and HO scale trains.

►This diagram compares the sizes of the scale gauge combinations most commonly used today. The different model sizes are known by a letter or number, such as 1, O, HO and N for example. Different countries have adopted differently sized scales and gauges which sometimes have the same name. This can make things difficult if you want to buy foreign models.

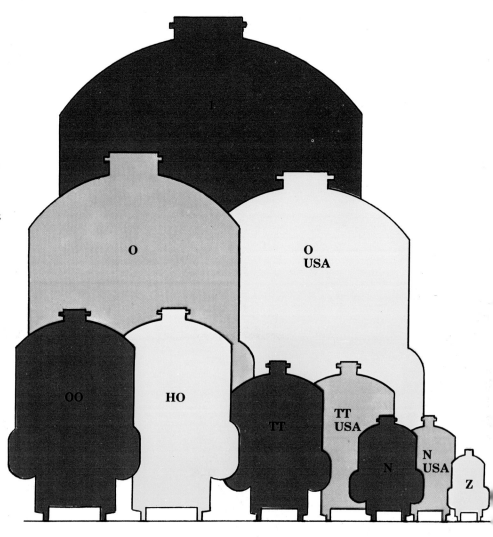

◄Clockwork trains were very popular until the 1940s when most homes became supplied with electricity. Some clockwork models were rather poor quality but many were sophisticated and well-made. Many people now collect and operate old clockwork trains. This gauge O locomotive was made in the 1920s.

▼Electricity is the most obvious choice for powering models today. There are large ranges of ready-to-run locomotives and rolling stock available in several sizes. You can also power accessories such as signals and turnouts with electricity. Electric trains do not have to be re-wound or re-fuelled as clockwork and live steam models do.

Clockwork trains have to be wound up with a key.

This chart shows the most common commercial model sizes used today. It gives their names, measurement and the countries in which they are most used.

GAUGE NAME	COUNTRY	TRACK GAUGE	SCALE RATIO	REMARKS
1	GB USA Europe	45mm	32:1	This very large gauge was widely used until 1920 and is now used mostly outdoors.
O	GB Europe	32mm	43:1	O gauge was the first which was really small enough to be used in the average house. It was very popular in the 1930s. A few manufacturers still make O gauge models and track.
O	USA	32mm	48:1	
HO	Europe USA	16.5mm	87:1	HO stands for "Half O" and it is the most popular model size in the world. It is slightly smaller than OO scale although both OO and HO models use the same gauge width and so can run on the same track.
OO	GB	16.5mm	76:1	OO gauge developed as real British trains were smaller than European and American trains and so were easier to model at a scale slightly bigger than HO.
TT	GB Europe	12mm	101:1	The letters TT stand for "Table Top", and indicate that this scale is convenient for indoor layouts as it is smaller than OO and HO. This scale is not much used now.
TT	USA	12mm	120:1	
N	GB	9mm	148:1	This was the first sub-miniature scale, developed in the 1960s and now the second most popular in the world, as it needs so little space.
N	Europe USA	9mm	160:1	
Z	World	6.5mm	220:1	Z gauge is really tiny and not widely available.

RAILWAY THEMES

Real railways are built to carry people and goods from one place to another. They pass through every kind of landscape and serve the needs of cities, ports, farms, quarries, and factories. Giving your model railway a theme and purpose to work to can make it seem more realistic and more fun to operate.

Three types of railway themes are illustrated here, with some of the trains that are likely to be run on them. The theme that you choose will affect not only the railway's scenery and shape, but also the sort of trains you buy and the way you run them.

Train information

A train is made up from rolling stock – passenger carriages, freight wagons, mail vans, repair vehicles and so on – and a powered locomotive which moves the train along the track. Locomotives and rolling stock are usually sold separately for you to put together in trains, according to the services you want to run on your railway. Models of different makes may have different kinds of couplers, so make sure that locomotives and rolling stock are compatible if you want to run them together.

When choosing models in a shop you will have to decide whether you want models of steam, diesel or electric locomotives. There will also be a wide range of liveries covering different times, countries, areas and railway companies. Most modellers decide on a time and area to model and make up trains from locomotives and stock that would have been used by the real railway. If you decide that you would like a variety of trains, there is no reason why you should not have them, but they may not look very realistic if run at the same time.

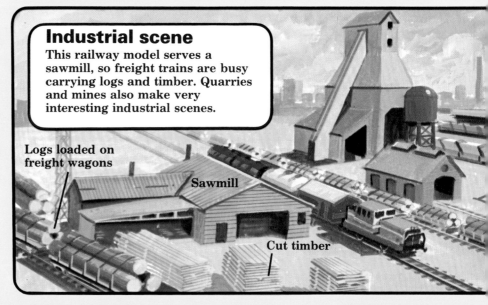

City station

This kind of main line city station gives you the chance to model interesting buildings and create a varied track system for lots of kinds of trains.

Work
po

Glass platform shelters

Industrial scene

This railway model serves a sawmill, so freight trains are busy carrying logs and timber. Quarries and mines also make very interesting industrial scenes.

Logs loaded on freight wagons

Sawmill

Cut timber

Country line

A country railway will give you the chance to make a lot of scenery and to run express trains, stopping services and goods trains on the same layout.

Passenger
foot bridge

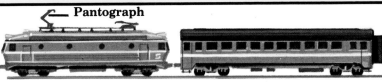

Pantograph

electric
es

▲This is an HO model, made by the Austrian firm Ro-Co, of an Austrian State Railway's electric express train. This locomotive has a working pantograph which picks up electric current from overhead power wires.

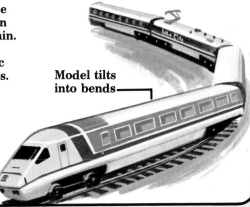

Model tilts into bends

►British Rail's latest high speed express is the Advanced Passenger Train (APT). This OO gauge Hornby model is designed to tilt, just like the real train, as it speeds round curves in the track.

►This sort of modern diesel locomotive would be very useful for shunting freight on an industrial layout, or for powering a goods train. Most model manufacturers produce a general purpose locomotive like this.

Closed goods vans

▼Although this German Railways steam locomotive is hauling a load of logs, it could also be used on a passenger service. The German company of Märklin produce this model in HO gauge, with working headlights.

Open wagons loaded with logs

Ploughed farm land

Observation coach

▲ Touring trains often pass through country holiday areas. This Arnold N gauge model of the famous Trans Europ Express (TEE) is pulling coaches used by the travel company "Apfelpfeil".

►This OO gauge model of the "Caerphilly Castle" is produced by the British firm Airfix. This steam locomotive provided a fast passenger express service in the 1930s.

This tender carries the engine's coal.

LAYOUT PLANNING

When you have decided on the power, scale and theme of the model railway you want to build, you are ready to plan it out in detail. You have to decide what size to make it, where you are going to put it and whether or not it can be permanently left in place when not in use.

If you are making your first model railway, it is a good idea to buy some track plan booklets. These provide lots of tested layout plans, and show you exactly which track pieces to buy and where to lay them. Many also give instructions on wiring and operating the layout for the best results.

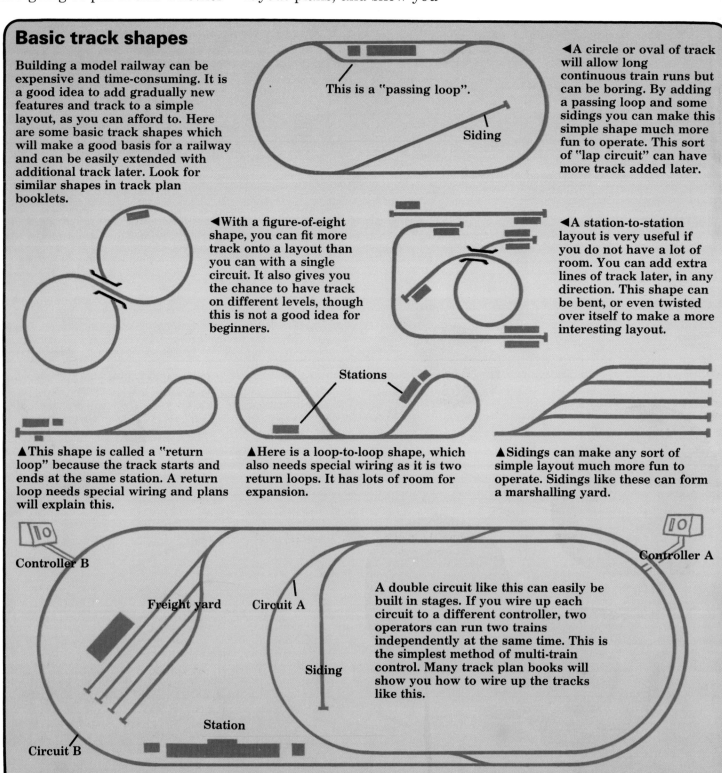

Basic track shapes

Building a model railway can be expensive and time-consuming. It is a good idea to add gradually new features and track to a simple layout, as you can afford to. Here are some basic track shapes which will make a good basis for a railway and can be easily extended with additional track later. Look for similar shapes in track plan booklets.

This is a "passing loop".

Siding

◄A circle or oval of track will allow long continuous train runs but can be boring. By adding a passing loop and some sidings you can make this simple shape much more fun to operate. This sort of "lap circuit" can have more track added later.

◄With a figure-of-eight shape, you can fit more track onto a layout than you can with a single circuit. It also gives you the chance to have track on different levels, though this is not a good idea for beginners.

◄A station-to-station layout is very useful if you do not have a lot of room. You can add extra lines of track later, in any direction. This shape can be bent, or even twisted over itself to make a more interesting layout.

Stations

▲This shape is called a "return loop" because the track starts and ends at the same station. A return loop needs special wiring and plans will explain this.

▲Here is a loop-to-loop shape, which also needs special wiring as it is two return loops. It has lots of room for expansion.

▲Sidings can make any sort of simple layout much more fun to operate. Sidings like these can form a marshalling yard.

Controller B

Controller A

Freight yard

Circuit A

Siding

A double circuit like this can easily be built in stages. If you wire up each circuit to a different controller, two operators can run two trains independently at the same time. This is the simplest method of multi-train control. Many track plan books will show you how to wire up the tracks like this.

Station

Circuit B

Track testing

Make sure that your trains can run properly on your track by testing a train on the layout before you pin the track into place permanently.

Pencils taped to side of train leave marks on the baseboard.

▲Trains hang over the edge of the track when they are running. To mark the width of this overhang, tape two pencils to your largest train and push it over the tracks. This will help you to judge how close to the track you can position scenery, other lines of track and railway accessories.

Back of tunnel

▲Make sure that any tunnels are tall enough and wide enough for trains to travel through. Leave the back of the tunnel open so that you can reach inside in case of accidents.

▲Test raised track to check it is not too steep for trains to climb. If lines cross at different levels be certain there is enough clearance for your trains on the lower line.

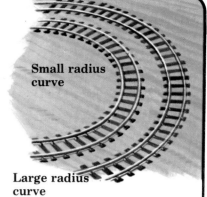

Small radius curve

Large radius curve

▲Trains must be able to pass each other on parallel tracks without touching. This is particularly important where the tracks are curved. If you are using "set-track" (bought ready-shaped) the outer track will be a "large radius" curve and the inner track a "small radius" curve. Make sure the curves are not too sharp for trains to travel round.

Railway building timetable

If you are making your first model railway layout, you may find it difficult to know where to start. Look around local model shops and buy lots of manufacturers' catalogues. These illustrate not only model locomotives and rolling stock, but also track, electrical equipment, buildings and accessories.

The list below will give you some idea of the stages in which you can tackle making a model railway. Do not try to be too ambitious on a first project. Pick a simple plan and add to it gradually. It is better to have a small layout in working order than a large one that takes months to build and wire up. Most model railways are never finished but are always being extended and changed in some way.

1 Choose a scale, gauge and method of power.
2 Look at the space available for your railway and decide on its shape, size and whether it can be left in position permanently.
3 Decide upon a railway theme.
4 Look in plan books for a plan that suits the scale size and purpose of your railway. Making your own plan is more difficult.

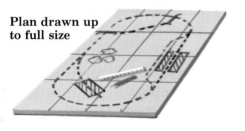

Plan drawn up to full size

5 Draw up your plan to full size. Most manufacturers produce templates specially for this job, that are the same shape and size as the curves, turnouts, crossovers and other sections of their set-track.
6 Draw scenic features such as woods, rivers, hills, roads and buildings on to this full-size plan.

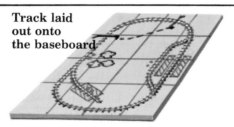

Track laid out onto the baseboard

7 Make the baseboard (see pages 18 and 19 for ideas on sizes and materials to use).
8 Lay the track out on the baseboard to check that it fits, then test-run a train round the layout as this will show up any running problems.
9 Drill holes in the baseboard next to the track for the electrical feed wires.

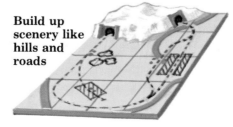

Build up scenery like hills and roads

10 Remove the track and build up the surface of the baseboard to create the hills, rivers, roads, tunnels, raised track and so on.

11 Paint the scenery and add surface texture materials, including track ballast or underlay on track routes.
12 Pin track firmly into place and connect up the electrical feed wires.

Paint the scenery and pin track in place

13 The railway is now in working order and you can operate trains while gradually adding extra track, scenery and buildings to the layout.
14 Don't be afraid to change your railway layout. You can re-route tracks, change the location of buildings and scenery and perhaps get rid of parts you no longer want. You can easily change the whole theme of the railway by replacing existing features with new ones. You can even extend the railway by building another board and joining it to the original one.

HOW MODEL TRAINS WORK

The majority of model railways today are powered by electricity. These pages explain how an electric model locomotive works and show the principles behind electrifying the layout. The main picture shows a typical model train controller, wired to a line of track and a cut-away view of a model's motor.

Most makes of model locomotive run on a 12 volt electric current, so the electricity supplied to your home will be too strong to use directly. It has to pass through a controller which reduces the current to a maximum of 12 volts. This low voltage is quite safe and there is little danger of it causing a fire or giving a serious shock.

Controllers are so called because they control the speed and direction of the model locomotives. They work rather like a tap, by regulating the flow of the electric current to the motor. When the power is increased, by moving the control knob or lever, the locomotive can travel faster. If the power is decreased it slows down.

The controller also changes the mains electric current from A.C. (alternating current) to D.C. (direct current), as models can only work on direct current.

Direction control knob

Speed control knob

− +

Positive wire joined to near rail.

Negative wire joined to far rail.

This wire connects the controller to the mains electricity supply.

Most electrically powered things, such as lamps and fires, are connected directly to the power supply. Model locomotives, however, are different. The electric current is fed to the rails which become live and the locomotive picks up the power as it travels over them. This is similar to the system used by some real electric railways.

The 12 volt D.C. current is fed from the controller to the rails of the track. The positive wire is joined to one rail and the negative wire to the other rail. The rails act like extensions of the wires, and carry the electricity. One becomes positive and the other negative. The rails are electrically isolated from each other, this means that no current flows between them.

Power circuit

Electricity has to flow in a complete and unbroken circuit. For instance when you wire up a light bulb to a battery, you have to use two wires as the battery has two terminals, one positive and one negative. The current flows from the battery along the positive wire to the bulb, and then back to the battery along the

negative wire. This is the electrical circuit.

The same principle applies in the electrification of model railways. The circuit runs from the controller to the positive rail, through the motor and then back along the negative rail to the controller. This circuit will only be complete when there is a locomotive standing on the track.

Electricity flows along the rail, into the motor, and then out and back to the controller.

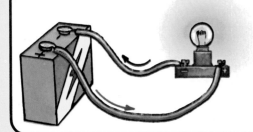

Inside a model motor

① The positive electric current in the near rail is picked up by the front, right-hand wheels of the locomotive. The back right-hand wheels are insulated by a thin covering of plastic, so they do not pick-up any electricity.

② The current is then carried along a connecting wire from the wheels to the locomotive's electric motor. The power passes through a series of carbon brushes to some coils of wire wrapped around a piece of metal. This is the armature and it becomes magnetized when current passes through the coils of wire.

③ The motor contains a permanent magnet which reacts with the magnetized armature, making it spin round and round very fast.

④ The armature is connected to the wheels by a drive shaft, so when it spins the wheels turn and move the locomotive. Most models also have a series of gears which help them to stop and start smoothly.

⑤ When the electricity has passed through the motor it is fed to the back left-hand wheels and goes out into the negative rail. It then flows along the rail back to the controller, so that it completes an electrical circuit (see picture on previous page below).

Permanent magnet

This is a picture of a model of a French diesel-electric, multi-purpose locomotive, with one side cut away to show the motor.

Drive shaft and gears

Armature

Connecting wire

The sleepers are made from non-conducting material so no current can flow between the two rails.

Positive rail

Reversing a train

Engine just travels backwards if it is turned round.

To change the direction of travel of a locomotive you must change the polarity of the rails. This means that the positive rail must become negative and the negative rail positive. Most controllers have a lever labelled "direction", which will do this automatically. If you were to simply turn the locomotive round it would run in the same direction but travel backwards.

11

WIRING UP YOUR LAYOUT

In order to run electric models on a layout you have to supply the rails with electric current. This is done by connecting the train controller (which is plugged into the mains supply) to the rails with pairs of "feeder" wires.

A small oval or circle of track will only need one pair of wires but larger and more complicated layouts may need a lot of wiring. It is a good idea to buy a track plan or booklet with clear instructions to help you wire up your first layout. These pages illustrate some of the basic principles of wiring.

Electrical resistance

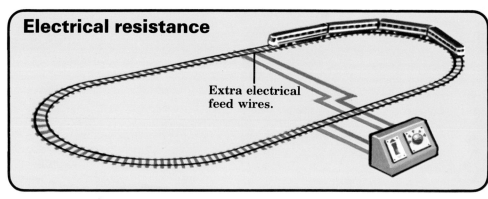

Extra electrical feed wires.

▲If you find that your trains are travelling more slowly as they move away from the controller, this shows that you need extra electrical feed wires. The locomotives are slowing down because the voltage of the electric current drops as it travels along the rails. This is called electrical resistance.

To prevent this voltage reduction fix extra feeder wires to the track, as shown above. These will increase the voltage and keep the trains travelling at a constant speed.

Overhead power

Some models of overhead electric trains are produced with working pantographs, so they can be run on a model "catenary" system as shown here. In most cases the power is picked up by the pantograph but completes the circuit back to the controller through the rails.

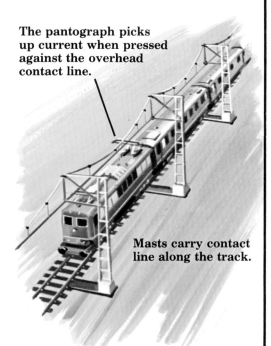

The pantograph picks up current when pressed against the overhead contact line.

Masts carry contact line along the track.

You can also buy locomotives with dummy pantographs if you want to power the locomotive through the rails in the usual way.

Block wiring

If you put two trains on one layout they will travel in the same direction and at similar speeds because they receive the same electric current.

This can be overcome by dividing the layout into sections that are electrically isolated from each other. The trains can then be independently controlled by turning the current on and off in the sections as each train passes through. You need one operator and one controller to drive each train.

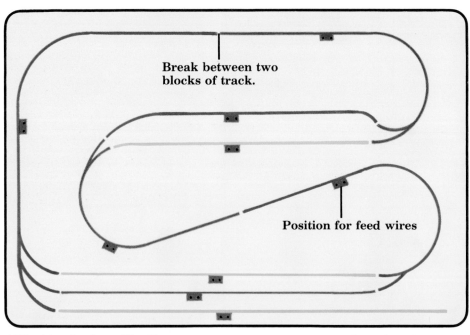

Break between two blocks of track.

Position for feed wires

▲Most track plans, like the one above, show you where to divide the layout and position the feed wires for this sort of wiring. It is often called "block wiring" or "cab control".

The blocks are created by cutting the track as no electrical current will pass over a gap, or by using the ready-made track isolators produced by some manufacturers.

Most turnouts (points) are self-isolating, which means that the current only flows along the line of track that the train will travel along.

Power clips

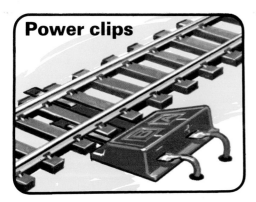

▲You can connect feeder wires to the rails in several different ways. The easiest, but most expensive, is with clip-on connections, pictured above. Many manufacturers produce these power clips and you can buy them in model shops.

Soldered connections

Make sure you fix all the positive wires to one rail and all the negative wires to the other.

Strip plastic covering from the feed wires and solder the bare metal to the metal rails with a modeller's soldering iron. *If the sleepers are plastic take care not to melt them.*

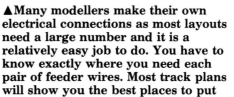

▲Many modellers make their own electrical connections as most layouts need a large number and it is a relatively easy job to do. You have to know exactly where you need each pair of feeder wires. Most track plans will show you the best places to put

the wires.
   Mark the feed positions on the baseboard and drill small holes on the outside of the track. Pull the feed wires through these holes and solder one wire to the outside edge of each rail, as pictured above.

Each block has to be wired up with two feed wires in the usual way, but it also has to be connected to two (or more) controllers so that either can supply current to the block. This means that there can be quite a lot of wiring to do if you have a lot of blocks. It is fairly easy to do, as it is the same process for each isolated block.

▼The easiest way to connect the two controllers to the blocks of track is by using "toggle switches", as described below.

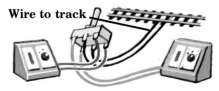

Wire to track

   The two controllers are connected to the switch which is wired to the track.

A   B

When the toggle is pushed to the left, controller A supplies power to the block. When it is pushed to the right

controller B supplies power. No current flows when the switch is in the centre. You need one toggle switch for each isolated block. With this system it is impossible for both controllers to power the same block at once.

▼You can build the toggle switches into a useful control panel like this. It shows the track layout, divided into isolated blocks with the appropriate toggle switch mounted in the middle of each block. The two controllers stand by the panel as they are both

wired to all the toggle switches. This layout can run two independent trains at the same time as there are two controllers. No matter what kind of layout and control you have, you always need one driver for every independent train.

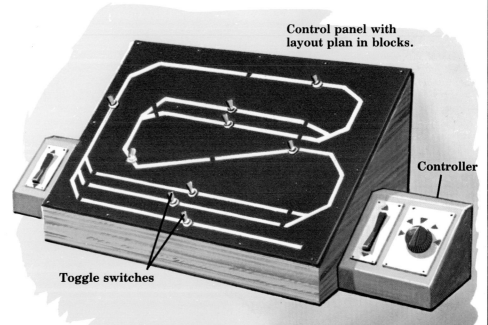

Control panel with layout plan in blocks.

Controller

Toggle switches

Operating cab control

Each train is controlled by one operator using one controller. The train's speed and direction are regulated by the controller in the usual way. The operator turns on the current, block by block, along the

chosen route using the toggle switches. When a train leaves a block the operator returns the toggle for that block to the off position, to show that the block is now free for the other train.

COMMAND CONTROL

The newest and most advanced way to power and run a layout is known as command control. There are several slightly different systems, produced by various manufacturers, but they all work on the same principles, using micro-processors.

Command control costs more than conventional control but it is easier to wire up and is more realistic in operation as several trains can be run independently at the same time.

The master unit

This is the master unit. It is plugged into the mains electricity supply and connected to both rails of the track in the same way as a conventional controller.

This new system, however, feeds the rails with a constant supply of 20 volt A.C. current. It does not control the trains by varying the voltage of electricity in the rails, as an ordinary controller does.

The master unit contains a micro-processor which acts like a tiny computer. By entering commands into the unit's keyboard, you can control the speed and direction of the locomotives.

The micro-processor sends a coded command along the rails, which only the chosen locomotive can pick up.

The micro-processor has a "memory" so it is able to carry on sending commands to the first locomotive while you enter commands for another. This means that several trains can run independently and simultaneously.

One is controlled by the operator and up to three, running over pre-set routes, by the master unit. Some systems allow up to four operators and 16 trains to work at one time. It would need a big layout and careful route planning to cope with so many trains and drivers.

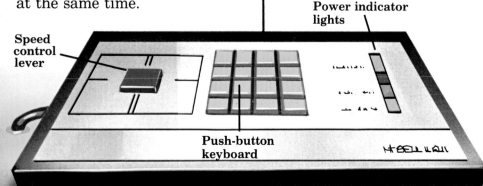

Speed control lever

Power indicator lights

Push-button keyboard

This ability to run several trains on one layout at the same time, yet with independent control of each, is command control's main advantage over more conventional systems.

Train modules

Locomotives can only be run on command control if they are fitted with a micro-chip module. These modules pick up the coded commands sent by the master unit. Each module has its own individual code and will only obey commands with the same code. You will have to fit the modules inside the locomotives yourself, but this is easy to do. Be sure to use modules of the same make as the master unit.

Inter-City 125

Some systems have a second kind of module which can be fitted to powered accessories, such as signals and turnouts. This makes wiring easier and operation more realistic.

RAILWAY MAINTENANCE

Maintenance is as important on a model railway as it is on a real one. If you look after your track and trains it will save you time and money later.

Model locomotives are designed to need only occasional simple home maintenance, such as oiling. If a locomotive breaks down, send it to the local service dealer for that make who will have the special tools and instructions needed for repairs.

If you try to mend it yourself you may make the fault worse. *You should never attempt to mend electrical equipment, such as a controller, as this could be very dangerous.*

Keep your locomotives clean. Fluff can get inside the motor if they are not put away in boxes after use.

Take care not to over-oil your locomotives as the oil will attract dirt, get on to parts of the motor that should be dry and make the track greasy.

Use only light lubricating oil, available from model shops.

Screws to hold body of this locomotive to the chassis.

▼The carbon brushes in your locomotive's motor will wear out and need replacing. Put in new brushes when the old ones are worn down close to the metal arm. For most makes of model this is an easy job that you can do yourself. The brushes are held against the motor by the spring clip. As they wear down the spring clip continues to push them against the motor until they wear out.

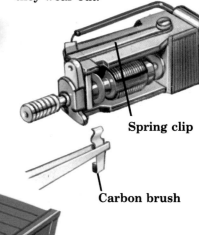

Spring clip

Carbon brush

Rolling stock usually requires little maintenance. A tiny drop of oil on the wheel bearings will make sure that wagons run smoothly.

Wheel bearings

Track cleaning

Check the track carefully before and after every operating session to make sure that it is level and firmly in place. Dirty rails will prevent the locomotives picking up maximum power. You can clean rails with a soft cloth and a little methylated spirit, or with a special abrasive rubber cleaning block. Some manufacturers produce rail-cleaning wagons which remove dirt as they travel over the track. The one pictured here is made by the German company of Fleischmann.

Soft cleaning pads rotate and rub against rails.

TRACKS

Like real trains, model trains have to run on track and it must be properly laid to give good running conditions. Many model manufacturers produce their own track, so if you buy more than one brand make sure that they can be used together.

There are two basic types of track, flexible track and set-track. Flexible track is more expensive and more difficult to use. Set-track is especially useful if you are following a published plan as this will tell you which pieces you need and show you where to put them and how to wire them up.

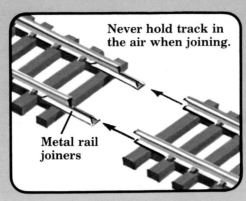

Never hold track in the air when joining.

Metal rail joiners

▲Both kinds of track come in standard lengths that have to be joined up with rail joiners (often called fishplates). Fix the joiners to one length and hold both tracks flat. Then gently slide the rails of the other length of track into the joiners.

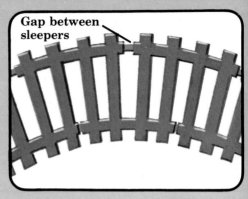

Gap between sleepers

▲Flexible track can be bent and curved to any shape because there are small gaps in the sleeper supports. When it is curved the two rails become uneven in length and the longest side has to be trimmed with a small razor-saw.

Changing tracks

Unless your layout is a very simple circle or oval of single track, you will need to have a variety of track pieces which allow trains to change directions and to cross from one line of track to another.

If you are using a layout plan it will tell you exactly which components you need and show you where and how to fix them together on the layout.

Track pieces such as turnouts and diamond crossings are sold ready-made, even for use with flexible track. These track pieces are very complex and difficult to make, so they are expensive. They are also delicate and easily damaged so take extra care when laying them. This is also important as trains are most likely to become derailed when travelling over crossings, turnouts and other track junctions.

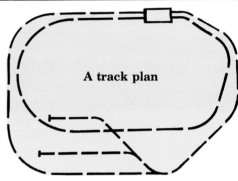

A track plan

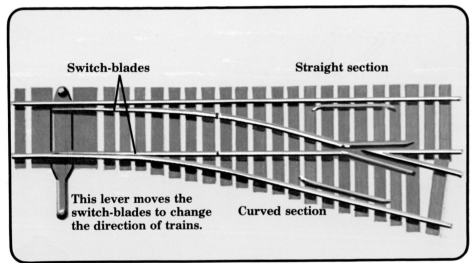

Switch-blades

Straight section

This lever moves the switch-blades to change the direction of trains.

Curved section

▲This is a turnout, also called a point or switch. A turnout is a straight section of track joined to a curved section. It is used to control which line of track a train travels along at a junction of two lines. This is done by moving the switch-blades so that one line of track is closed off

and only the other can be used.

Turnouts can be operated by tiny motors, but these are quite expensive and need to be wired up for power. It is cheaper to use small hand-operated levers, fixed on the baseboard next to the turnout. Turnouts can be curved either to the left or the right.

▲This is an automatic model turntable, powered by a small motor fixed to the underneath. Turntables rotate and are used to turn trains round to face the opposite direction and to put trains onto a particular line of track. They are mostly used on old-fashioned steam railways.

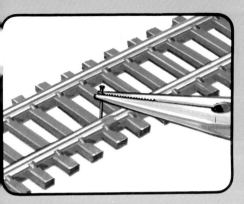

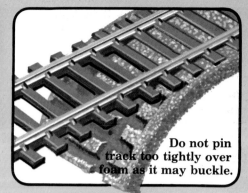

Do not pin track too tightly over foam as it may buckle.

▲Track is fixed to the baseboard with tiny track pins. Most track has holes already drilled in it for the pins. Never push the pins in too hard, they should just hold the track firmly in place. Small pliers are the best tool for this job, as a hammer could harm the track.

▲Real railway tracks rest on a bed of stones called ballast. Model ballast not only looks realistic but also reduces the noise made by models. You can buy model ballast chips in model shops. It should be stuck down on a bed of glue before fixing the track into

place. Brush off all loose ballast before pinning down the track.

Another way of modelling ballast is by using strips of foam or cork. This has indentations for the track to lie in and is stuck into place before fixing the track down.

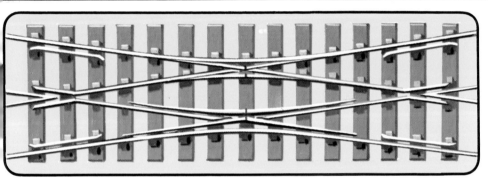

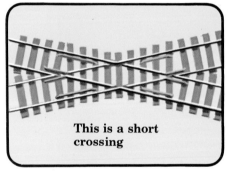

This is a short crossing

▲This complex piece of track is called a double-slip. It acts rather like a pair of turnouts joined together, as it allows not only for two lines of track to cross, but also for trains to change from one line to the other at the junction.

This sort of sophisticated device is more expensive than an ordinary turnout or crossover, as it is more difficult to make. You can also buy three-way turnouts, which feed three lines of track into a single line.

▲This is a diamond crossing. It is a junction of two lines of track, but it does not enable trains to cross from one line to the other – you need a double slip to do this. You can buy long or short diamond crossings.

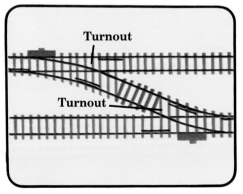

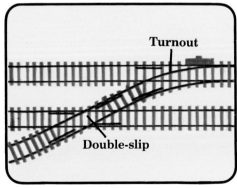

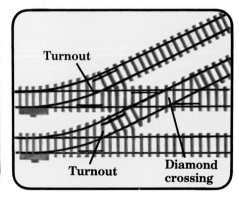

▲This is a "crossover" which enables trains to change from one track to another. It is made up from two turnouts. You can have a "facing crossover" which the train drives over forwards, or a "trailing crossover" which it backs over.

▲This is a single junction, where one line of track joins up to two lines of track. To make this single junction, you have to fit one left-hand turnout and one double-slip. Trains from the single line can go on either of the other lines.

▲Here, two lines of track join two other lines, forming a double junction. This is made up from two turnouts and one diamond crossing. If you are using a published track plan it will tell you exactly which parts to buy.

BUILDING BASEBOARDS

Whatever kind of railway layout you have planned, it must be built on a firm, strong baseboard. When the trains are running, they can cause enough vibration to make the scenery and track become loose unless fixed to a steady surface.

You should construct your baseboard carefully, as it will quickly become impossible to run any trains if the baseboard is warped or wobbly.

If you are lucky you will be able to build a layout in a room in your house or in a dry shed or garage and leave it up when it is not in use. Most people do not have enough space for a permanent railway and make portable baseboards which can be kept in a cupboard or under a bed when not being used.

The frame of the baseboard should be firm and strong as it has to support the weight of all the scenery you build up on it and carry the load of the running railway.

Make the frame from lengths of softwood, such as pine. Put cross braces in two directions at intervals of about 30cm (12in). This will strengthen the frame and keep it straight. Glue and screw all the joints together, making sure that they are straight and at right angles first.

Track beds

Once you have made the baseboard you should put any raised tracks or roads into place. They can be made from scrap wood and left-over pieces of surface board, as shown below. Make sure that the track beds do not rise too steeply or your trains may not be able to climb up them. Check also that they are very firm and do not wobble.

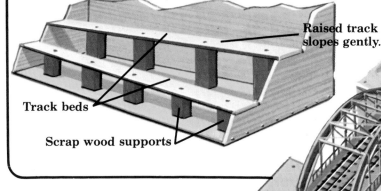

Raised track slopes gently.

Track beds

Scrap wood supports

Surface board such as wood fibre insulation board.

Corner bracket helps to keep corners square and firm.

Flat-headed nails

Softwood timber

Cross brace

Joining baseboards

If you want to make a large, but portable layout it is a good idea to build it on several smaller boards, rather than one huge one. You can join two boards together with large bolts, as shown below and in the main picture. To make the join even firmer, put a catch or hinge along the side, as pictured on the right.

Hinge has a removable pin, which is inserted when the boards are put together.

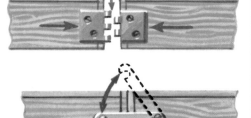

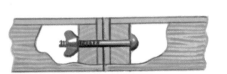

Bolts for joining baseboards together.

If you are joining baseboards together with two bolts, drill holes in both the frames at once, before putting on the top surface. This will ensure that they fit together well.

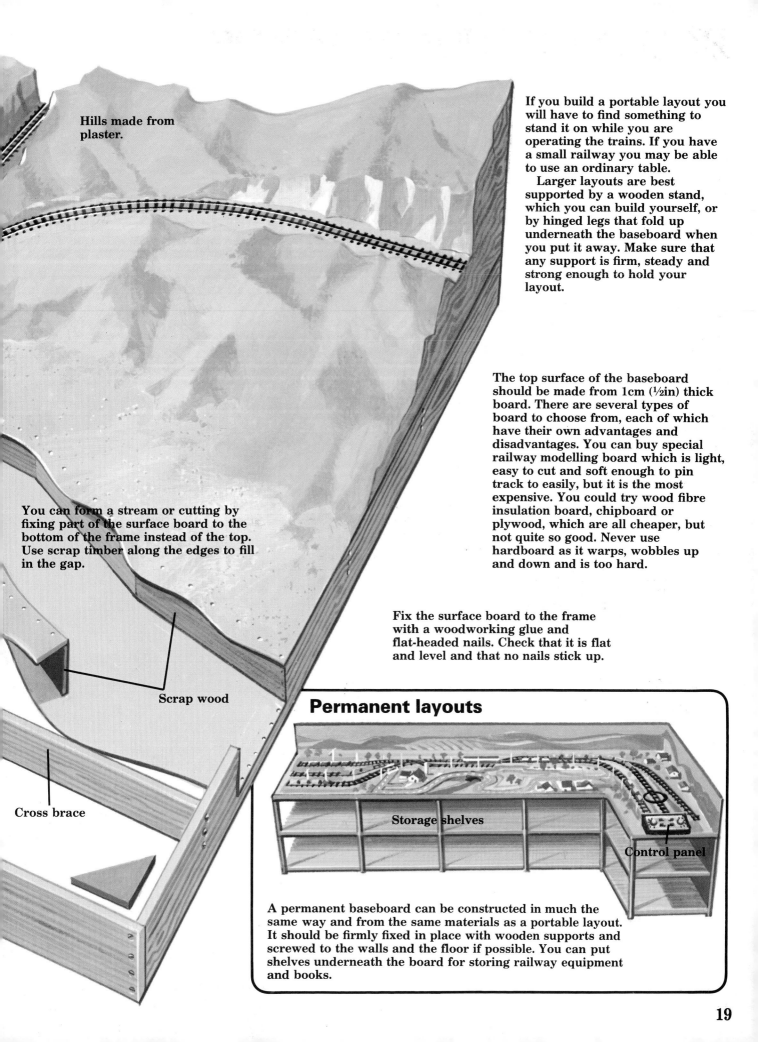

Hills made from plaster.

If you build a portable layout you will have to find something to stand it on while you are operating the trains. If you have a small railway you may be able to use an ordinary table.

Larger layouts are best supported by a wooden stand, which you can build yourself, or by hinged legs that fold up underneath the baseboard when you put it away. Make sure that any support is firm, steady and strong enough to hold your layout.

The top surface of the baseboard should be made from 1cm (½in) thick board. There are several types of board to choose from, each of which have their own advantages and disadvantages. You can buy special railway modelling board which is light, easy to cut and soft enough to pin track to easily, but it is the most expensive. You could try wood fibre insulation board, chipboard or plywood, which are all cheaper, but not quite so good. Never use hardboard as it warps, wobbles up and down and is too hard.

You can form a stream or cutting by fixing part of the surface board to the bottom of the frame instead of the top. Use scrap timber along the edges to fill in the gap.

Fix the surface board to the frame with a woodworking glue and flat-headed nails. Check that it is flat and level and that no nails stick up.

Scrap wood

Cross brace

Permanent layouts

Storage shelves

Control panel

A permanent baseboard can be constructed in much the same way and from the same materials as a portable layout. It should be firmly fixed in place with wooden supports and screwed to the walls and the floor if possible. You can put shelves underneath the board for storing railway equipment and books.

BASIC SCENERY

When putting scenery on your layout you have the choice between buying ready-made accessories and building your own. Most modellers do both, buying things which are difficult to make. It is a good idea to experiment and practise making model scenery. The following six pages illustrate some of the methods and materials that you can use to make hills, trees, ponds and buildings.

Shaping hills

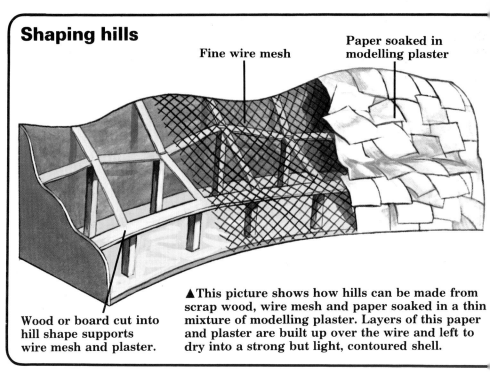

Fine wire mesh

Paper soaked in modelling plaster

Wood or board cut into hill shape supports wire mesh and plaster.

▲This picture shows how hills can be made from scrap wood, wire mesh and paper soaked in a thin mixture of modelling plaster. Layers of this paper and plaster are built up over the wire and left to dry into a strong but light, contoured shell.

Painting and texturing

This picture shows how a realistic effect can be achieved on a layout with paint and the addition of texture to the surface of scenery. All natural surfaces are rough and this look can be modelled by scattering tiny granules over the surface of your layout. Sand, sawdust, fine gravel, coal dust and dried tea leaves are all suitable. By experimenting you will find many other things that are useful too. You can buy "scatter materials" in a wide range of colours from model shops.

See page 23 to find out how to make trees.

For a ploughed field make grooves in damp plaster with a pointed matchstick or a comb. When it has dried, paint the plaster muddy brown and sprinkle sand, sawdust or scatter material over the wet paint. The paint will hold the texture in place. Another way of getting this effect is to use corrugated card instead of plaster.

This part of the layout shows how the scenery looks when texture material has been added.

This section of the layout has been painted but does not have very much surface texture, so it looks rather flat and unrealistic.

Here is the bare, plaster shell as it appears before painting. Texture can easily be added at this stage by roughening the plaster before it has fully dried.

This sort of fence is easily built from old matchsticks and cotton.

A rough track looks effective on a country layout. Carve ruts, tyre tracks and puddles in damp plaster and paint it a mixture of muddy grey colours. Coal dust will look like tarmac, and the puddles can be filled with glue, which looks like water when set.

Crumpled newspaper can be removed when lint or scenic mat is glued into place.

If you use lint put it with the fluffy side up and colour it green.

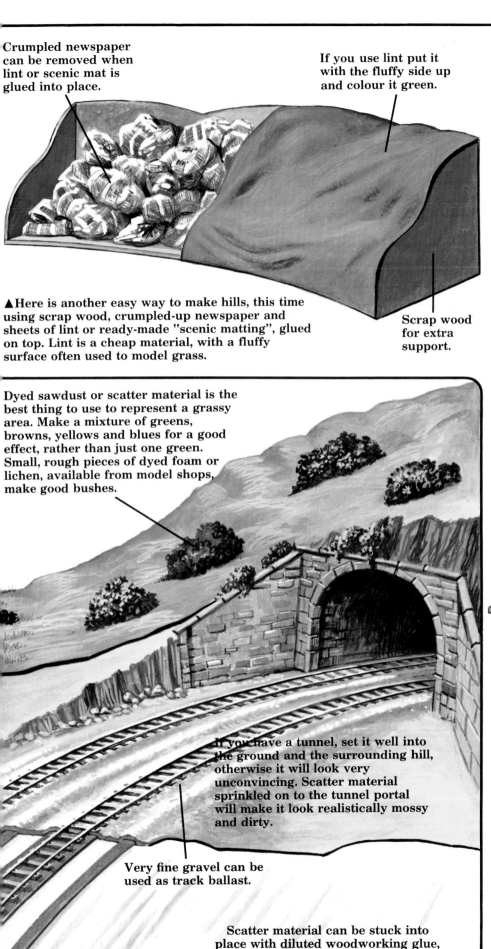

▲Here is another easy way to make hills, this time using scrap wood, crumpled-up newspaper and sheets of lint or ready-made "scenic matting", glued on top. Lint is a cheap material, with a fluffy surface often used to model grass.

Scrap wood for extra support.

Dyed sawdust or scatter material is the best thing to use to represent a grassy area. Make a mixture of greens, browns, yellows and blues for a good effect, rather than just one green. Small, rough pieces of dyed foam or lichen, available from model shops, make good bushes.

If you have a tunnel, set it well into the ground and the surrounding hill, otherwise it will look very unconvincing. Scatter material sprinkled on to the tunnel portal will make it look realistically mossy and dirty.

Very fine gravel can be used as track ballast.

Scatter material can be stuck into place with diluted woodworking glue, paste or even wet paint.

▲Solid plaster would be much too heavy to use for making hills on most layouts, but polystyrene is ideal as it is very light and strong. It can, however, be hard to shape and is melted by some kinds of glue and paint. Emulsion and poster paints are safe to use.

Rock faces

▲This picture shows how to get a realistically rocky effect by pressing crumpled tin foil onto damp plaster. Peel it away once the plaster has set hard.

▲Tree bark or cork can also make a good rock face. You can buy cork at florists or model shops.

▲To get the effect of long grass press some green dyed lint, fluffy side down, on to damp plaster or glue. After it has dried pull the lint away. The fibres will stick to the surface and give the impression of long grass.

MAKING TREES...

You can buy model trees ready-made and in kits to put together. These tend to be relatively expensive, so it is cheaper to make your own. On this page we show some of the methods of model tree building.

For the best effect, vary the sizes of the trees and do not put them into regular positions.

▼ The easiest and cheapest way of making model trees is to glue some lichen, shredded foam rubber or dried tea leaves onto real twigs. Paint the finished model and sprinkle a little scatter material over it for a mossy, leafy effect.

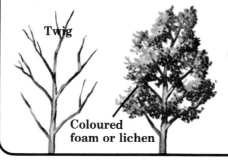

Twig

Coloured foam or lichen

Use a hand drill to twist the wire tightly.

Paint the finished tree.

▲Another method is to unravel some string into threads, cut it into short lengths and lay it along a loop of thin wire. Twist up the wire very tightly so that it forms a bottle brush shape. Fluff out the string and trim to shape.

A good way of making realistic, detailed trees is from thin wires twisted together to form a trunk, then gradually unwound to make ever smaller branches.

1 Cut some lengths of multi-stranded wire, a little longer than you want the tree to be when finished.

2 Wrap the lengths of wire around a nail and fix in place with some tape. This forms the trunk of the tree.

3 Pull out the wires to form big branches. Then gradually unwind the wires in each branch to make smaller branches.

Tape

Paint bark greyish browns.

Nail used to secure tree in place.

4 Once each wire branch is fully unwound along its length, the single strands of wire will look like little twigs.

5 Cover the trunk and branches with tape and then a rough layer of plaster to form "bark".

6 Make the leaves from bits of coloured lichen or shredded foam rubber. Stick the foliage into place with watered down white, woodworking glue.

7 The finished tree can be painted a mixture of greens and brown colours.

Forests and woods

If you want a lot of trees on your layout, you do not have to make each one individually but can create a forest or wood as a whole. The best position for a wood is against a backboard on the edge of the layout.

Make a row of individual trees to stand at the front, using whichever method you prefer. Build-up a slope from the front row of trees to the backboard, using scrap wood, wire mesh and plaster. Then cover the wire mesh with lichen or whatever you have used to make leaves on the front row of trees. It should now look like the tops of trees growing on a hillside.

Lichen or other material to represent leafy tree tops.

Wire mesh to support lichen

Scrap wood support

Plaster

Individual trees

Paint background a dark colour so it will look like the interior of a wood.

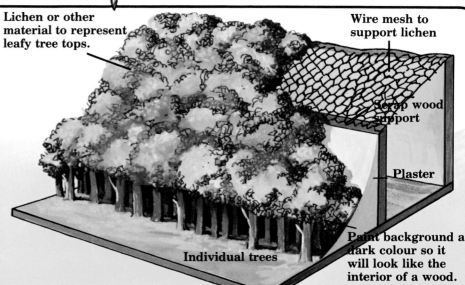

...AND WATER

The kind of water that you model will depend upon the theme of your layout – a city scene is more likely to have a canal than a waterfall, for instance. There are several methods of modelling water, each creating a different effect, so use the way which seems best.

Streams

▶One of the easiest ways to model water is to shape it out of the damp surface plaster of the layout. You can mould it into waves and ripples and use tiny stones to represent rocks sticking up out of the water. Paint the plaster with a blend of several colours as this will look more natural than one bright blue. Paint the centre a little darker to give an impression of depth. Finish off with several coats of shiny varnish for a wet look. This method is very good for modelling waterfalls and fast flowing rivers and streams.

Sea

▶Glass can give a good effect if you want to show a large body of water like a pond, lake or the sea. You can buy sheets of glass, moulded on one side into a ripple pattern. Position the glass about 1 cm (½ in) above the bottom of the lake. Paint the flat underside of the glass with a blend of colours making it lighter close to the bank so that it looks like shallow water.

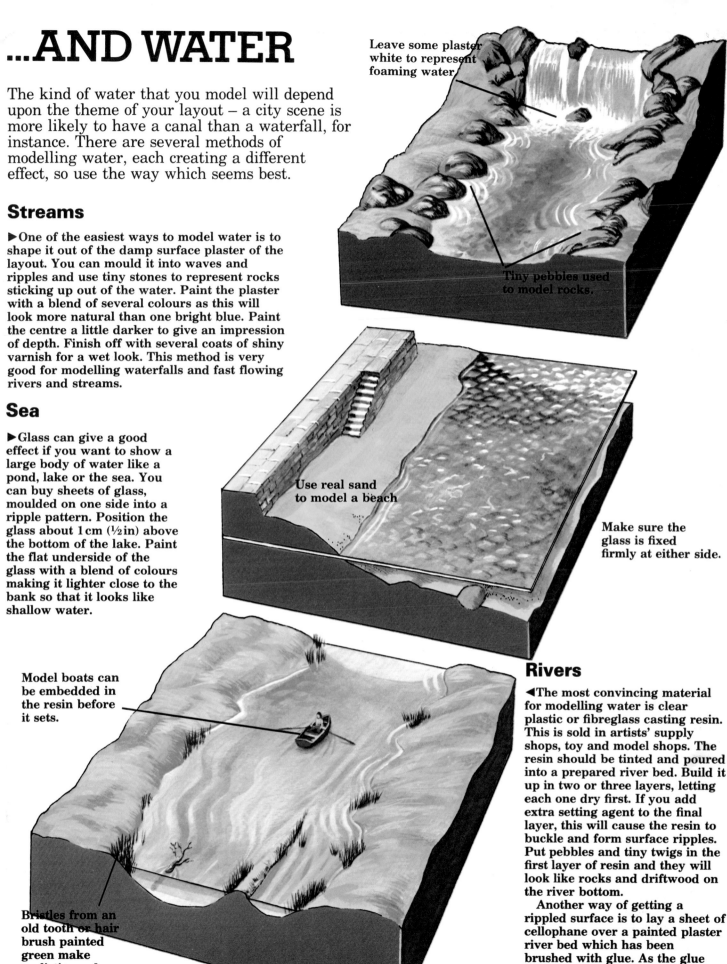

Leave some plaster white to represent foaming water

Tiny pebbles used to model rocks.

Use real sand to model a beach

Make sure the glass is fixed firmly at either side.

Model boats can be embedded in the resin before it sets.

Bristles from an old tooth or hair brush painted green make realistic reeds.

Rivers

◀The most convincing material for modelling water is clear plastic or fibreglass casting resin. This is sold in artists' supply shops, toy and model shops. The resin should be tinted and poured into a prepared river bed. Build it up in two or three layers, letting each one dry first. If you add extra setting agent to the final layer, this will cause the resin to buckle and form surface ripples. Put pebbles and tiny twigs in the first layer of resin and they will look like rocks and driftwood on the river bottom.

Another way of getting a rippled surface is to lay a sheet of cellophane over a painted plaster river bed which has been brushed with glue. As the glue dries it will make the cellophane crinkle.

MAKING BUILDINGS

Model buildings are an important part of any scene, but especially on town layouts. A large range of model buildings can be bought ready-made, either painted or unpainted, and many model manufacturers produce kits that you can construct at home. Make sure that the buildings are the right style and scale for your layout.

You can also make your own buildings from scratch, using a variety of commercial materials such as printed brick or stone paper, modelling clay and plastic sheeting embossed with a brick or stone pattern. All buildings are basically box shaped, and this is the first thing to make, using thick card for the walls, floors and roof. Once you have this basic box, cut out spaces for the doors and windows and

glue printed paper or embossed plastic on to the plain walls to get a brick or stone effect. Windows and doors are best built separately and then glued into place on a building.

The picture below shows an exploded view of an old-fashioned, British country station and illustrates some of the methods and materials that can be used to make buildings of any type.

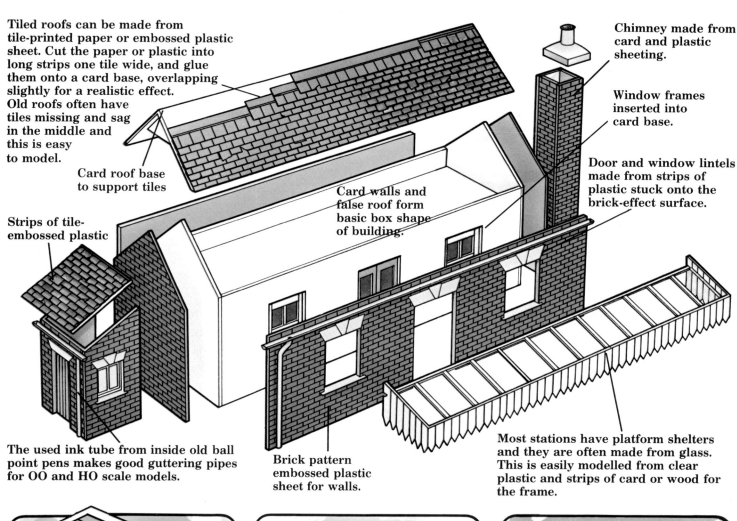

Tiled roofs can be made from tile-printed paper or embossed plastic sheet. Cut the paper or plastic into long strips one tile wide, and glue them onto a card base, overlapping slightly for a realistic effect. Old roofs often have tiles missing and sag in the middle and this is easy to model.

Card roof base to support tiles

Strips of tile-embossed plastic

The used ink tube from inside old ball point pens makes good guttering pipes for OO and HO scale models.

Card walls and false roof form basic box shape of building.

Brick pattern embossed plastic sheet for walls.

Chimney made from card and plastic sheeting.

Window frames inserted into card base.

Door and window lintels made from strips of plastic stuck onto the brick-effect surface.

Most stations have platform shelters and they are often made from glass. This is easily modelled from clear plastic and strips of card or wood for the frame.

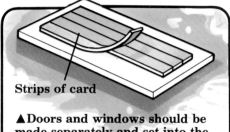

Strips of card

▲Doors and windows should be made separately and set into the walls rather than glued in place flat. Simple wooden doors can be made from strips of card, glued on to a card base, as shown in the picture above.

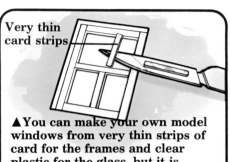

Very thin card strips

▲You can make your own model windows from very thin strips of card for the frames and clear plastic for the glass, but it is difficult to do well. Ready-made windows are sold by many model shops.

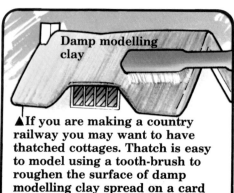

Damp modelling clay

▲If you are making a country railway you may want to have thatched cottages. Thatch is easy to model using a tooth-brush to roughen the surface of damp modelling clay spread on a card roof base.

Low-relief modelling

If you are putting buildings at the edge of your layout, you can save time, money and space by making only part of the buildings and placing them against a back-drop. This is called low-relief modelling and it can look very effective when used to build a whole street of houses. One ordinary commercial model building kit can make up to three or four low-relief buildings.

If you do put up low-relief buildings, you will have to make a backdrop board to lean them against. This can be made out of any kind of wood or board and then painted to represent sky and distant scenery. You could try gluing photographs cut out of magazines, or a commercially printed picture sheet, to the backboard if you want to show a more complex scene, like a town.

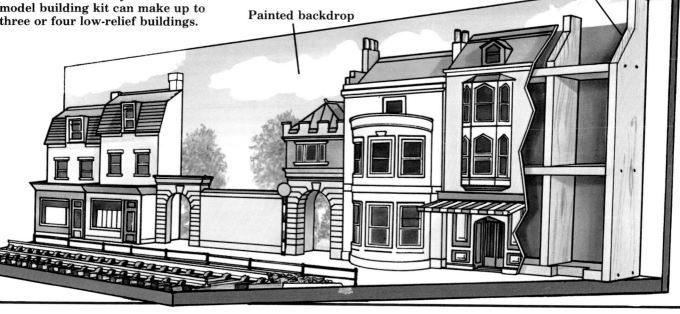

Painted backdrop

Wooden frame supports low-relief buildings made from card and brick paper.

Painting and weathering

The easiest and most dramatic way to improve unconvincing buildings (ready-made and home-made) is by painting them to look weathered. Weathering can be applied to any part of the scenery and even to the model trains themselves.

Most ready-made materials are uniform in colour but they can be made to look realistic by picking out some bricks or stones in varying shades of the base colour. Bricks often have patches of white "bloom" which can be modelled by rubbing a small patch of white paint on to the model.

Buildings in towns and close to railway lines are usually very dirty. Rubbing a little ash or putting a diluted wash of brownish-grey paint over parts of your models will make them seem realistically dirty.

If you have an old fashioned layout with steam trains, put smoke marks on bridges that trains pass under.

Train is painted to look dirty and well-used.

Colour of bricks has been varied.

Paving stones made from grey card or plastic sheet.

RAILWAY OPERATION

The way in which you operate your model railway will depend a great deal upon the layout's theme, size and the sort of trains that you have. For example, if you do not have any sidings or freight wagons you will find it difficult to carry out shunting operations.

The best way to decide on the kind of services and trains you would like to operate is by finding out how real railways work. There are lots of different things that you can try out with your model railway. This picture illustrates and explains some of the services that you could run, showing how different kinds of trains are made up and operated.

Express passenger trains travel very fast along the main lines and make few stops. They are run at regular intervals and have right of way on the track. The train is made up from a powerful locomotive and may even be double-headed.

They are usually long trains, with lots of corridor coaches, some of them first class, there is often a buffet or restaurant car too.

Trains run at night will have several sleeping compartments and there may also be a mail sorting van in which mail is sorted by postmen during the journey.

Express freight trains are also long fast trains powered by a powerful locomotive. They deliver perishable or urgent goods, such as food and chemicals and have right of way over slower trains.

These trains often haul a load made up of just one commodity and are usually non-stop along the main line. They are less frequent than other trains so there may be one a day, or only one a week.

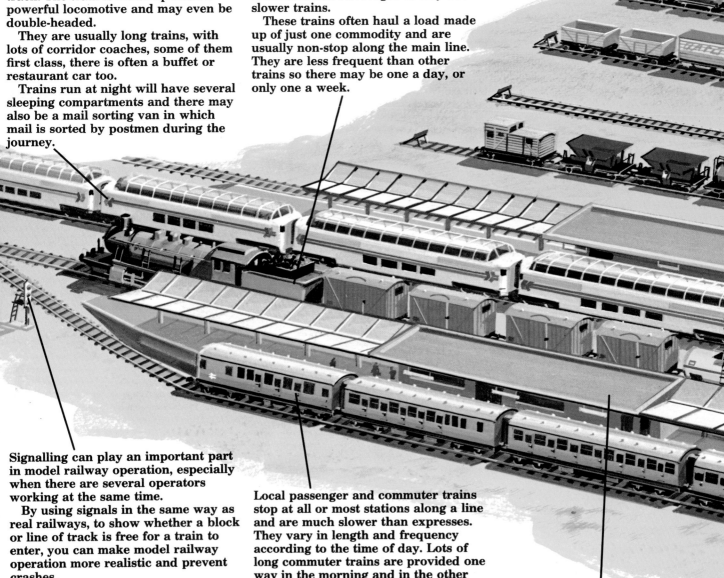

Signalling can play an important part in model railway operation, especially when there are several operators working at the same time.

By using signals in the same way as real railways, to show whether a block or line of track is free for a train to enter, you can make model railway operation more realistic and prevent crashes.

Model railway layouts are sometimes used by real railway companies to teach signalmen and other employees about signalling and other railway procedures.

Local passenger and commuter trains stop at all or most stations along a line and are much slower than expresses. They vary in length and frequency according to the time of day. Lots of long commuter trains are provided one way in the morning and in the other direction in the evening.

Trains run in the day will be less frequent and smaller. Coaches are likely to be non-corridor and all one class. The locomotive will be smaller and less powerful than those used on expresses. Modern trains are likely to be a multiple-unit (see page 31) like the one seen waiting in the passing loop here.

With imagination you can make a single station on your layout represent every station along the main line between two big cities. Express trains rush past it and local trains stop every time they reach it.

Timetables and scale-time

Most real railways operate their trains to a scheduled timetable. You can easily devise a simple timetable for your model railway to provide various freight, express and passenger services.

Lots of modellers go one step further and run their timetable to a "scale-time", often a ratio of one real minute equalling 12 scale-minutes. Scale-time can make train operation seem more authentic. By working at the 1:12 scale-time ratio, a five (real) minute model run becomes a long journey lasting one scale-hour.

Operating a model railway to a scale-time timetable can be great fun but it is also very difficult to organize, especially if you are operating alone on a small layout.

Practise with a slower scale-time ratio and an extremely simple timetable to start with. Don't forget that you must have one operator for each locomotive moving on the layout. It is only possible to run a complicated timetable on a large layout worked by several operators.

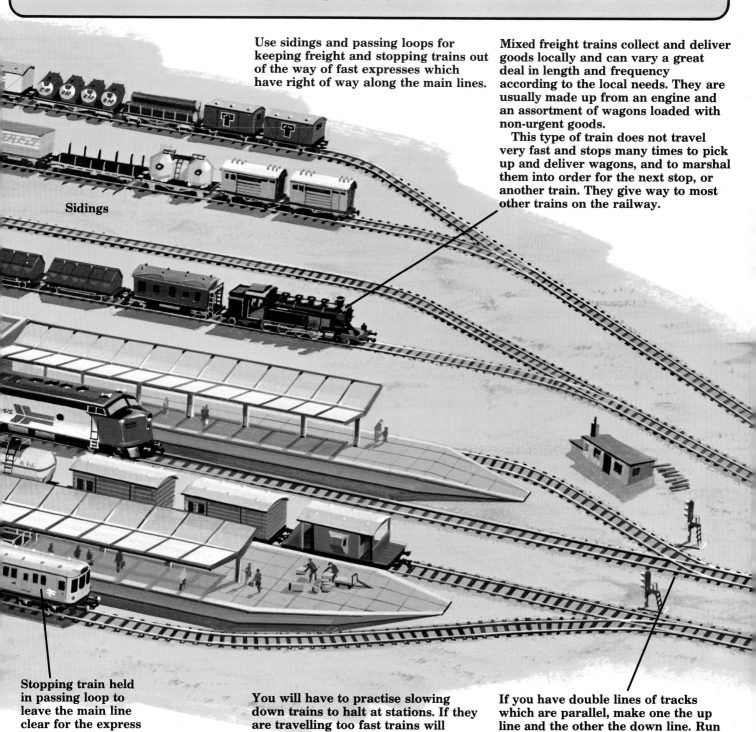

Use sidings and passing loops for keeping freight and stopping trains out of the way of fast expresses which have right of way along the main lines.

Sidings

Mixed freight trains collect and deliver goods locally and can vary a great deal in length and frequency according to the local needs. They are usually made up from an engine and an assortment of wagons loaded with non-urgent goods.

This type of train does not travel very fast and stops many times to pick up and deliver wagons, and to marshal them into order for the next stop, or another train. They give way to most other trains on the railway.

Stopping train held in passing loop to leave the main line clear for the express freight train.

You will have to practise slowing down trains to halt at stations. If they are travelling too fast trains will overshoot the station and have to reverse back. Sudden stops look very unrealistic and can lead to trains becoming derailed.

If you have double lines of tracks which are parallel, make one the up line and the other the down line. Run trains in the appropriate directions at all times as this will make operating easier and much more authentic and stop accidents.

VINTAGE LOCOMOTIVES

Model trains have been popular since the middle of the 19th century when real railways were first developed. Early models were not small-scale replicas of real trains, as modern models are. They were quite large and often made from brass, iron or wood. Very old models, such as these, are now rare and extremely valuable.

You could start your own vintage model collection by looking for "tin-plate" models made between about 1900 and the late 1950s.

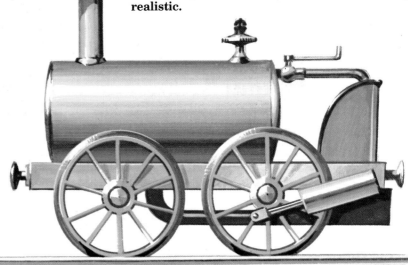

▼This brass locomotive is typical of the early models produced in the mid 19th century. They were live steam engines, fuelled by methylated spirit and often known as "dribblers" because they left a trail of dirty water behind them. Although well made, this sort of model did not look very realistic.

▼Towards the end of the 19th century the dribblers began to be replaced by more efficient and realistic looking models, like the one pictured here. They were made from brass and powered by a model steam engine. By today's standards they seem very large as they were about three or four times as big as modern OO/HO scale.

▼Many early model trains were simple toys and not powered in any way. They did not run along tracks but were pushed or pulled along the floor. This picture shows a brightly coloured, wood and paper floor train. Models like this were especially popular in America during the pioneer days.

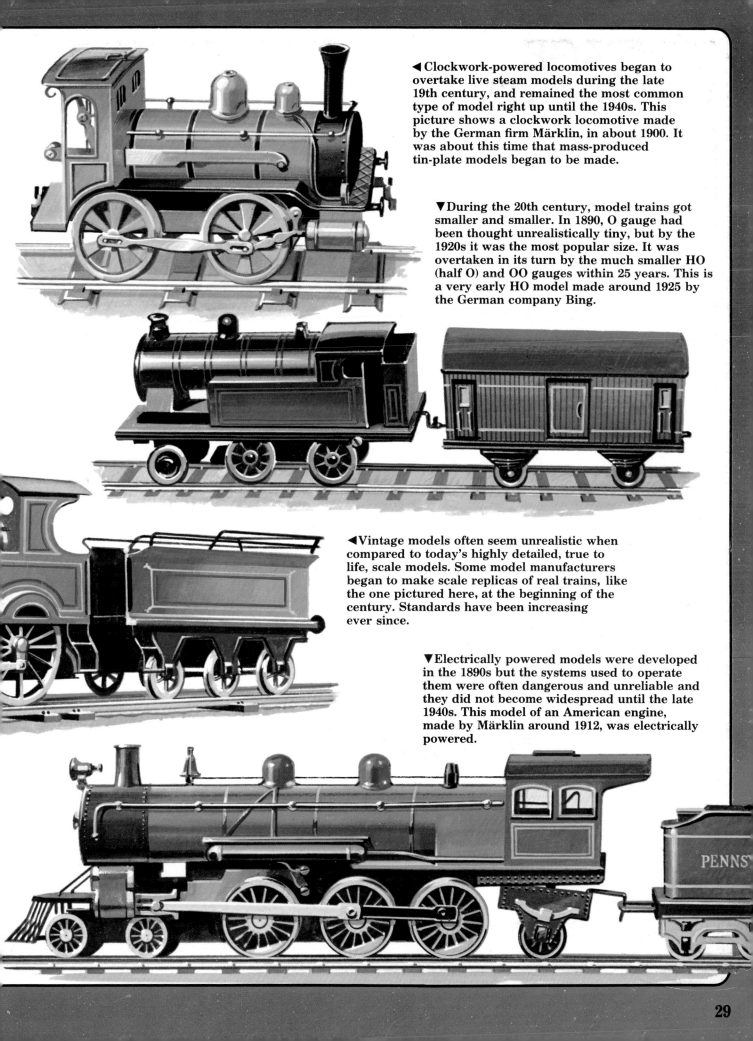

◄Clockwork-powered locomotives began to overtake live steam models during the late 19th century, and remained the most common type of model right up until the 1940s. This picture shows a clockwork locomotive made by the German firm Märklin, in about 1900. It was about this time that mass-produced tin-plate models began to be made.

▼During the 20th century, model trains got smaller and smaller. In 1890, O gauge had been thought unrealistically tiny, but by the 1920s it was the most popular size. It was overtaken in its turn by the much smaller HO (half O) and OO gauges within 25 years. This is a very early HO model made around 1925 by the German company Bing.

◄Vintage models often seem unrealistic when compared to today's highly detailed, true to life, scale models. Some model manufacturers began to make scale replicas of real trains, like the one pictured here, at the beginning of the century. Standards have been increasing ever since.

▼Electrically powered models were developed in the 1890s but the systems used to operate them were often dangerous and unreliable and they did not become widespread until the late 1940s. This model of an American engine, made by Märklin around 1912, was electrically powered.

TRAIN WORDS

When you begin railway modelling you will hear lots of new words and technical terms which you may not have come across before. This glossary explains some of the more common words, most of which are also used for real trains and railways.

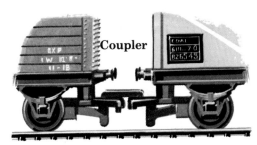

Coupler

Ballast – a foundation of small stones on which the track and the sleepers are laid.
Banking – assisting a train by putting extra locomotives to push it from the rear.
Baseboard – a supporting frame and top board on which the model railway is built.
Bogie – pivoting wheel base at either end of a long wagon which enables it to go round sharp curves.

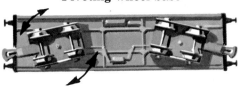

Pivoting wheel base

Branch line – a minor line which serves an area off the main line.

Cab control – sometimes called block wiring, this system allows independent control of more than one train on one layout at the same time.
Caboose – a guard's van at the end of the train (American term).

Carriage – a passenger-carrying vehicle.
Catenary – the cable used in overhead electric power systems (see page 18).
Coupling – method of connecting vehicles together to form trains.

Diesel locomotive – a locomotive powered by an internal combustion engine that is fuelled by diesel oil.
Double-headed train – an extra long or heavily loaded train that needs two locomotives to power it.

Double-headed diesel train

Engine – another, and more common, name for locomotive.
Express train – a train that gives a very fast, often non-stop, service to passengers and freight.

Fiddle-yard – storage sidings which are part of the model layout, but hidden from view.
Fishplate – another name for a model rail joiner.

Gauge – the distance between the inside edges of the rails. This word is also used when describing the different sizes of models, as in HO gauge (see pages 4 and 5).

Halt – a small stopping place on a local railway line that does not have full station facilities.

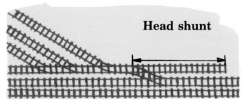

Head shunt

Head shunt – a line of track that is joined to and runs parallel to the main line. It has sidings running off and is used for shunting to leave the main line free.

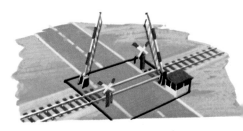

Level crossing – used where a road and railway line cross.
Light engine – a locomotive that is running without a train.
Local line – a line where passenger trains stop at every station.

Main line – this is a major route used by express trains that do not stop at every station.

GOING FURTHER

Modular railways

An increasingly popular method of building railway layouts is the modular system, where individuals make portable layouts that can be joined together to form one large railway. The individual layouts have to be built within certain defined limits and these are set-out in official manuals. There are two modular systems, one for N gauge railways called NTRAK and one for HO gauge railways called HOtrak.

Club news

Many areas have model railway clubs, whose members meet regularly to build and operate model railway layouts. They often build highly detailed railways specially for exhibitions.

Club layouts are usually quite large because there are a large number of modellers willing to work on them. You may find it very helpful to join a club and learn about railway modelling from experienced modellers. Your local model supply shop will probably be able to tell you where and when the nearest club meets.

Most countries have a national model railway club or association which organizes exhibitions, competitions and acts as a governing body for the hobby.

GREAT BRITAIN:	The M.R.C. (Model Railway Club)
U.S.A.:	The N.M.R.A. (National Model Railroad Association)
AUSTRALIA:	The A.M.R.A. (Australasian Model Railway Association)
NEW ZEALAND:	The N.Z.M.R.G. (New Zealand Model Railway Guild)

Marshalling yard – an area of sidings where wagons are shunted to form trains.

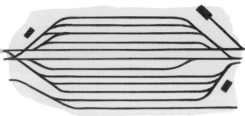

Multiple unit – a train with a motorized coach at either end. They are either electrically powered (EMUs) or diesel powered (DMUs). The motorized coaches have a driving cab.

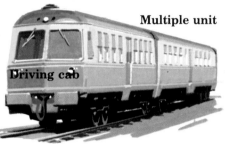

Multiple unit

Driving cab

Pantograph – an attachment fixed to the top of an electric train that picks up electric current from overhead electric power wires.

Prototype – a modelling term for the real thing on which a model is based.

Point – a piece of track that directs trains from one line of track to another. Also called turnouts or switches (see pages 16 and 17).

Shunting – the moving of coaches and wagons to form trains. This is usually done in sidings.
Shunter – a name given to a small locomotive used in sidings.

Sidings – lengths of track used for shunting and for storing wagons and locomotives when not in use.
Signals – are used to indicate if a line of track is free for a train to use. Modern signals are coloured lights. Old fashioned semaphore signals have a pivoting arm that is moved to show a line is clear.

Signal box – a building from where signals and points are controlled.
Sleepers – wooden or concrete beams fixed underneath the rails.

Tank locomotive – a steam locomotive that carries its own supply of fuel and water.
Tender – a type of wagon that is permanently coupled to a steam engine and which carries the fuel and water for the engine.

Tender

Terminal – a station at the end of a line of track.
Tie – an American word for sleeper.
Tin-plate – term used to describe old model trains made from tin-plate (see pages 28 and 29).

Uncoupler – a device fitted between the rails to automatically uncouple model trains.

Up line – the track that trains use when going towards the main terminal station. The down line is used by trains travelling away from the main station.

Wagon – a freight-carrying vehicle, can be open or closed.

Further reading

Books and magazines about railway modelling can be very useful but check that they tell you what you want to know. Some books concentrate on model trains, rather than on railway things in general. You may also find some ranges of information leaflets too complicated if you are a beginner, so look before buying.

Magazines are usually published once a month and often feature good pictures and descriptions of model railways. They also have useful reviews of new products and exhibitions. The many advertisements will help you to find out what is on the market and to decide what you want.

Books to read

The World of Model Trains. Patrick Whitehouse and Allen Levy. (Bison)

The Encyclopedia of Model Railways. Terry Allen. (Octopus)

The World of Model Trains. Guy R. Williams. (Andre Deutsch/Rainbird)

OO & HO Scale Model Railways. Michael Andress. (Almark)

Model Railway Basic Scenery. Michael Andress. (Almark)

Collectors Guide to Model Railways. J. Joyce. (Argus Books)

Magazines to read

GREAT BRITAIN:	Model Trains, Model Railways, Railway Modeller, Continental Modeller, Model Railway Constructor.
U.S.A.:	Model Railroader, Railroad Model Craftsman, Model Railway News, Trains.
AUSTRALIA:	Australasian Model Railway Magazine.

INDEX

First published in 1980 by
Usborne Publishing, 20
Garrick Street, London
WC2E 9BJ

© 1980 Usborne Publishing
Ltd.

The name Usborne and the device are
Trade Marks of Usborne Publishing Ltd.

We wish to thank
John Hills and M&R
(Model Railways) Ltd.,
for their assistance.

Printed in Belgium by Henri,
Proost et Cie, Turnhout,
Belgium.